Molly Bang

TEN, NINE, EIGHT

PUFFIN BOOKS

FOR DEBORAH,
PRESHIEL, SYLVIA, VIKI
AND THEIR CHILDREN
AND FOR
DICK AND MONIKA,
WITH THANKS
AND
LOVE

10
small toes all washed
and warm

9 soft friends
in a quiet room

8 square windowpanes with falling snow

7 empty shoes in a short straight row

6 pale seashells
hanging down

5 round buttons on a yellow gown

4 sleepy eyes which open
and close

3 loving kisses on cheeks and nose

2 strong arms around
a fuzzy bear's head

1 big girl all ready for bed